Inspector Drake's Last Case

A Comedy By
David Tristram

A Flying Ducks Publication

For more information on all Flying Ducks Publications, visit the website:

www.flyingducks.biz

ISBN 978 0 951 72677 8

A Note To The Director...

Inspector Drake's Last Case is designed to make people laugh - loudly and often. It's one of a series of adventures featuring the indomitable Drake, all of which have been thoroughly tested in front of audiences of all sizes and descriptions. Without exception, they lapped up the lunacies with a remarkable vigour.

This is also a very practical play. It requires just one room-set throughout and, even though the cast is perhaps larger than average, there's scope for doubling. The parts of Mary Ship and Mrs Gagarin could be played by the same actress, and the stretcher-bearers, who make just two fleeting appearances and say nothing, could easily double as your back-stage staff.

As I directed the original production, the script isn't heavily annotated. It's far more fun working out your own bits of business, and extending the comedy beyond words into slapstick visual routines.

Don't be afraid to break the rules - Inspector Drake's Last Case can accommodate your wildest ideas, and if they're funny, they're relevant.

Above all else, have fun.

D.T.

DRAMATIS PERSONAE
(The ones in the play)

MRS GAGARIN
MR GAGARIN (HER SON)
SERGEANT PLOD
INSPECTOR DRAKE
MISS DUCK
MR BUTLER (THE GUEST)
MR GUEST (THE BUTLER)
MR COOK (THE GARDENER)
MRS GARDNER (THE COOK)
MARY SHIP (THE VICAR'S DAUGHTER)
TWO STRETCHER-BEARERS (ONE MALE, ONE FEMALE)

A Flying Ducks Publication

PROLOGUE

Spotlight on Sergeant Plod.

Plod Evenin' all. You know, murder's a funny business. What drives a man, or woman, to kill another human being? Is it fear? Anger? Greed? Jealousy? Well, one thing's for sure. No-one could have foreseen the strange events that took place one dark Spring evening at the home of the elderly Mrs. Gagarin, and her son Victor. Indeed, it took the world's greatest detective to unravel the complexities of that foul, and most unnatural....MURDER! I hope the amateur sleuths amongst you will attempt to solve the crime, by piecing together the clues - which are right there, in front of your eyes. But if I might give you just a few tips - don't believe everything you see, don't always expect a murderer to tell the truth and, above all, make sure you know who's who.

The spotlight begins to dim.

Well, it's getting dark - just how it was that Spring evening as the elderly Mrs Gagarin was taking a stroll in her garden. Could she have known then, that she was about to become the subject of Inspector Drake's Last Case?

Total darkness. There is a burst of dramatic music.

ACT ONE FOLLOWS IMMEDIATELY.

A Flying Ducks Publication

ACT ONE

The stage is black. The silhouetted figure of Mrs Gagarin enters, front of curtains. She is carrying a lit torch, and moves slowly towards the other side of the stage.

Mrs Gagarin Hello? Who's there? I know there's someone there. Come on. Who is it? *(She points the torch directly at the audience for maximum darkness on stage)* Oh, it's you!

There is a gunshot. Mrs Gagarin screams. There are four more shots. The torch goes off. The stage is totally black. There is a burst of dramatic music, and the curtains open to reveal a crowded room. Mr Gagarin, Mr Butler, Miss Duck, Mr Guest, Mrs Gardner and Mr Cook are talking excitedly in groups. Sergeant Plod stands rigidly centre stage. Gagarin moves towards Plod. He walks with a severe limp, and with the aid of a stick.

Mr Gagarin How much longer will we have to wait, Sergeant?
Plod Inspector Drake will be here as soon as possible, sir. Try to be a little patient. *(There is a pause, then Plod begins to chuckle to himself)*
Mr Gagarin *(tersely)* Something amusing you, Sergeant?
Plod I was just thinking, sir. "Try to be a little patient" as the doctor said to the midget.
Mr Gagarin Forgive me if I don't join you in a hearty giggle, Sergeant, but my mother has just been shot dead.
Plod *(embarrassed out of his laugh)* No offence intended.

Nevertheless, after a pause, Plod begins to chuckle again, and this time is stopped by an agitated Miss Duck.

A Flying Ducks Publication

Miss Duck Can I go now, Sergeant?

Plod 'Fraid not, miss. The Inspector gave strict instructions that you all be kept in this room till 'e harrives.

Mr Gagarin What's he like, anyhow, this Inspector...er...

Plod Drake - the best, sir. Don't you fear, he's the best there is. And I should know, I've worked with them all - Miss Marple, Sexton Blake, Maigret, Dangermouse...

Miss Duck I'm very impressed, Sergeant. Next you'll be saying you've worked with Sherlock Holmes.

Plod Only in a strictly advisory capacity, Miss, but oh yes, in my time I've seen them all - but there's none to touch Inspector Drake.

Mr Gagarin The question is, can he find my mother's killer?

Plod Well, if he can't, no-one can. Never failed yet. It's his mind see, sir. So quick. Why, next to him, I'm like an imbecile.

Mr Gagarin *(dryly)* Really.

Plod True as I'm standing here. Can you imagine that, Miss?

Miss Duck I think so, Sergeant, yes.

Gagarin summons Duck to the front of the stage with a flick of his head.

Mr Gagarin We must talk. Try to look nonchalant. *(They instantly stand back to back)* Look, Alison, old stick, I think it might be wise if we played down our relationship in front of this Drake fellow.

Miss Duck *(puzzled)* What relationship?

Mr Gagarin That's the idea, old thing. After all, we both have a lot to gain from my mother's death, and our friend the Inspector might start to get the wrong idea.

Miss Duck We've nothing to hide.

Mr Gagarin Well of course not. But it's common knowledge that there was no love lost between mother and me, and, well, it seems silly to complicate the investigation.

Miss Duck Don't worry, Victor. Mum's the word.

Mr Gagarin Very droll, my sweet. Sergeant, where on earth is that Inspector of yours? We've been here almost an hour.

Plod I've told you once sir, he'll be here as soon as poss...shh! Why, I think I can hear Inspector Drake coming now!

They all stop and listen. There's a high pitched squeal of tyres, a car door shuts, footsteps hurry up a gravel path, and Drake enters. As he struts confidently towards

Mr Gagarin, he is striding inexorably towards a low hanging bed-warming pan.

Mr Gagarin Ah! Inspector...Duck!
Drake Drake!

As Drake reaches to shake Gagarin's hand he is floored by the impact of the pan on his brow.

Mr Gagarin I did try to warn you, Inspector - that low warming pan catches a lot of people out.
Drake *(recovering)* And you are?
Mr Gagarin Victor Gagarin. Mrs Gagarin was my mother.
Drake My condolences, Mr Gestapo.
Mr Gagarin Gagarin.

Drake is already wandering about the room, staring at everything, talking in a distracted manner. A momentary glance up the chimney leaves him with a blackened nose.

Drake Your mother, you say.
Mr Gagarin That's correct, Inspector.
Drake No point in lying to me over little things like that, eh, Mr Dustbin?
Mr Gagarin *(tense)* The name's Gagarin. Victor Gagarin!
Drake *(still wandering everywhere)* Yes, yes of course it is.

Drake spots a poker, and begins to examine it with a magnifying glass. A curious Plod leans over his shoulder and, noticing there's no lens in the magnifying glass, he pushes his finger through it, and into Drake's eye. Drake belts him on the helmet with the poker in childish retaliation. Drake hands the poker to Plod.

Get that fingerprinted.

Plod daubs the poker with his fingerprints. Drake begins to pace once more.

It must have been a great shock to find her dead.
Mr Gagarin Well, it was certainly unusual.
Drake What's that you're standing on?
Mr Gagarin *(looking down, bemused)* Those are my feet, Inspector.
Drake Make a note, Sergeant. We've got a comedian amongst us.

Plod *(scribbling in his notepad)* Sir.

Drake Now, let's start again. What's that you're standing on? The rug!

Mr Gagarin It's a rug.

Drake I see. Move your foot.

Mr Gagarin What?

Gagarin moves off the rug. Drake stoops to rub the rug with his finger. He then examines his finger.

Drake That's very interesting.

Mr Gagarin What is it?

Drake It's my finger. Sergeant, remove the rug for questioning.

Plod Sir!

Drake is standing with one foot on the rug, one off. As Plod begins to pull the rug, Drake's legs slowly begin to split.

Mr Gagarin How dare you! That's a valuable Persian rug.

Drake It could also be a valuable clue, Mr Grappling Irons. And you'll soon learn that nothing escapes my notice. Nothing. For instance, I've already noticed that you're getting taller...AARGH! *(Drake finally collapses backwards. Gagarin helps him to his feet)* Put the rug back, Sergeant.

Plod Sir.

Drake I'd like to start by questioning the staff.

Mr Gagarin *(looking at his walking stick)*   What, this old stick?

Drake The servants, Mr Growbag.

Mr Gagarin I see. Very well. *(Gagarin gives two claps. Cook, Gardner, and the hunchbacked Guest line up. Gagarin first points to Guest)* This here's the butler.

Drake Yes, I had a hunch you'd show up.

Mr Gagarin *(angrily)* Inspector Drake! Can we get on with it?

Drake The butler, eh? Look, if you did it you may as well tell me now. Save a lot of time. What's your name? *(There's no response from the deaf old butler. Drake tried again, louder)* I said "What's your name?" *(There's still no response)* Is this man still alive?

Mr Gagarin You'll have to use his ear trumpet.

Drake *(grabbing the trumpet and bellowing into Guest's ear)* BUTLER!

Mr Butler *(spraying sherry everywhere)* What is it, Inspector?

Drake Stay out of this. I'll come to you later.

A Flying Ducks Publication

Mr Gagarin Inspector, that's one of my mother's guests. His name is Butler.
Drake So what's the butler's name?
Mr Gagarin Guest.
Drake Make a note of that, Sergeant.
Mr Gagarin This is our gardener, Mr Cook.
Mr Cook How do you do.
Drake *(refusing a filthy handshake)* Delighted.
Mr Gagarin And this is our cook, Mrs Gardner.
Drake And what's your name, Mrs Gardner?
Mrs Gardner *(slightly bemused)* Mrs Gardner, sir.
Drake So there are two Mrs Gardners?
Mr Gagarin I think not, Inspector.
Drake Don't play games with me, Mr Gooseflesh. Sergeant, read back the list
  of suspects.
Plod Well sir, let me see. I've got Guest the butler, Cook the gardener,
  Gardner the cook and Butler the Guest.
Drake Mmm. And you are? *(He swings to face Miss Duck, and strides towards
  her)*
Miss Duck Duck! *(Drake instinctively ducks)* Alison Duck. What are you doing
  down there, Inspector?
Drake *(on his knees)* Examining your shoes, Mrs Duck.
Miss Duck *(with a flirtatious air)* Miss!
Drake *(he wipes a smear of mud from her heel onto his finger)* That's interesting.
  This mud on your heel - it's not the same colour as the mud in the garden.
Miss Duck No, that's dog pooh. I trod in it outside. Thanks for removing it.
Drake *(cheesy grin)* My pleasure.
Miss Duck I'm Mrs Gagarin's business partner. That's to say, she was mine.
Drake And exactly what line of business are you in, Miss Duck?
Miss Duck Clothes, Inspector. Fashion. I'm a designer. *(She twirls to show off
  her provocative dress)* Do you like it?
Drake *(a moment's uneasy pause)* Take that down, Sergeant.

*Plod's eager advance is halted as Duck stubs the cigarette on the end of her holder
into his groin.*

Mr Gagarin My mother provided the money to set up the business, Inspector.
  She too recognised Miss Duck's...talent.
Drake And you are?
Mr Gagarin Victor Gagarin - we have been introduced.

Drake Ah yes.

Drake breaks off to continue his study of the room, followed closely as usual by Plod. Gagarin beckons Duck to the front of the stage, and once again they stand back to back.

Mr Gagarin The man's an idiot.
Miss Duck I think he's rather cute.
Mr Gagarin He can't even get my name right.
Miss Duck He's had a nasty blow on the head.
Mr Gagarin Undoubtedly the least important part of his body.
Miss Duck Don't underestimate him. I bet he's already working on some ingenious theory. *(They break from the aside)* Inspector?
Drake *(his head pops up from behind the settee)* Yes?
Miss Duck Why do you think someone would want to murder a frail, defenceless, and disgustingly rich old woman?
Drake At this stage, Miss Duck, I'm guessing. But I think someone wanted her dead.
Mr Gagarin Er, yes Inspector. But why should someone want her dead?
Drake Let's not play with words, Mr Gibberish, this was murder - pure and simple.
Mr Butler I think what they're trying to say, Drake, old chap, is have you got any idea of the motive?
Drake Who the hell are you?
Plod *(referring hastily to his notes)* That's Butler, sir, the guest.
Drake *(turning to Guest)* And this must be Guest the butler.
Mr Gagarin Well done, Inspector!
Drake I'm getting the hang of this now. *(Shouting at Guest)* Right Mr Guest, what was your question again?
Mr Guest I don't have a question, sir.
Drake Don't waste my time, butler!
Mr Gagarin That's Guest!
Mr Butler I'm Butler!
Drake The guest?
Mr Butler That's right. And I said...
Drake *(shoving Butler brusquely aside)* I'll come to you later. *(Turning to Gardner)* Now, Mrs...er...(He strides towards the warming pan again)*
Mrs Gardner Duck!
Drake Mrs Duck...Ummmph! *(He is floored again)*

A Flying Ducks Publication

Mrs Gardner I did try to warn you, Inspector. That low warming pan catches a lot of people out.
Plod That's Mrs Gardner, sir, the cook.
Drake Well, of course it is. Now, Mrs Gargoyle.
Mrs Gardner Gardner.
Drake No, I'll come to him later. Tell me, how long have you been in the employ of Mrs Gritsniffer?
Mrs Gardner How long have I been in what, sir?
Drake How long have you been working for the old woman?
Mrs Gardner Oh. Up until she died.
Drake I see. *(He begins to pace again)* Question! Did Mrs Garbage Truck know who her killer was?
Mr Gagarin I should imagine she's the only one who did, Inspector.
Drake Precisely! And there's your motive!

A puzzled silence.

Miss Duck I'm sorry, Inspector, but that gazelle-like mind of yours seems to have left us all behind again.
Drake Forgive me. I sometimes forget that my brain works at a different speed from that of a normal person.
Mr Butler That's true.
Drake Well, it's obvious. Explain it to them, Sergeant.

A look of uneasy panic sets into the Sergeant's face. Finally, in desperation, he faints. The others rush to help him to his feet.

Miss Duck Are you all right, Sergeant?
Plod I just need a breath of fresh air. Excuse me.

Plod exits.

Drake Right, now try and stay with me. Mrs Glue Sniffer was the only one who knew who her killer was - right?
Others Right.
Drake So that's why he killed her - to shut her up!
Miss Duck But...until he killed her, there was nothing to shut her up for.
Drake You stick to making pretty dresses, Miss Duck. Leave the murder investigations to me.

Mr Gagarin So, you think he killed her, because she was the only witness to her own murder?

Drake Exactly! Ever thought of joining the Force, Mr Floor Gripper?

Mr Gagarin The name's Gagarin, Inspector. And if I ever have a frontal lobotomy, I'll let you know.

Enter Mary Ship, heavily disguised as a cleaning lady, armed with a hoover. No-one seems to pay any attention to her.

Drake Well, I've got a job to do, and we're going to go through this again and again until I get some answers. Now, I want all of you to tell me exactly what happened here tonight. Let's start with you, Mr Guest-Butler.

As Butler gets up, the hoover is switched on. The noise is deafening, and we hear nothing of Mr Butler's explanation to Drake. The audience is left to imagine what words could possibly accompany the outlandish actions - strangling gestures, piggy-back rides, etc - a story of incredible complexity and outrageous excesses. Finally, just as Butler sits down, the hoover is switched off and Mary Ship exits.

I see. So you noticed nothing unusual tonight? *(There is a murmur of agreement from the rest)* Is there anyone else in this house, apart from us here?

Mr Gagarin No-one.

Drake What about a cleaning lady - a maid or something?

Mr Gagarin I said there's no-one else here, Inspector.

Off stage we hear Mary Ship give a short scream, followed by a giggle and the words "You naughty boy!" Drake whips open the door, to reveal Plod, crouched in the doorway, looking guilty.

Drake Feeling better, Sergeant?

Plod Much better, sir.

Drake drags him in, and looks in vain behind the door for any sign of a woman. Frustrated, he begins to pace the room again, and stops in front of the grandfather clock, which has stopped at 10.03.

Drake Sergeant, what time do you make it?

Plod *(consulting his wristwatch)* Just after eleven, sir.

A Flying Ducks Publication

Drake This clock has stopped. *(He examines it, and produces a bullet)* Aha! A bullet! *(He goes over to the French windows, and begins to plot out a ridiculous looping trajectory for the bullet)* It must have strayed through the French windows during the shooting, Mr Globule.

Mr Gagarin I presume you're talking to me.

Drake How long has this clock been stopped like this?

Mr Gagarin *(consulting his wristwatch)* Well, as it's now just after eleven, I'd say about an hour.

Drake About an hour. Make a note of that, Sergeant. So the shooting must have taken place about...er...10 o'clock.

Mr Butler Three minutes past, I'd say, Inspector.

Drake You seem very well informed, Mr Buttocks.

Mr Butler Butler!

Drake No, I'll come to him later. Tell me, where were you at 10.03 precisely?

Mr Butler If you must know, I was playing bridge.

Drake Alone?

Mr Butler Of course not.

Drake Aha! And just how many others were with you?

Mr Butler Do you play bridge, Inspector?

Plod Just answer the Inspector's questions.

Mr Butler Three others. Mr Gagarin, Miss Duck, and...

Drake And?

Mr Butler And Mrs Gardner.

Plod Mrs Gardner's the cook, sir!

Drake The cook? Does the cook often play with the guests?

Mr Gagarin That was my idea, Inspector. You see, my mother was due to be the fourth player, but she had a headache, and said she preferred to go for a walk instead. So I asked Gardner, the cook, to be a guest.

Drake I see. You! Mr Cockroach.

Mr Cook Cook!

Drake No, I'll come to her later. Tell me, where were you at 10.03 tonight?

Mr Cook I was in cook's quarters.

Drake You were in your quarters.

Mr Cook No, I was in cook's quarters.

Drake You were in the quarters of the cook, Mrs Gamebird.

Mr Cook I was. She was fixing me a snack of tomato soup. When I heard the gunshot, I spilled some down my shirt.

Drake Yes, I did notice the stains. Sergeant - the shirt!

Plod unceremoniously rips the shirt from Cook's back, places it in a plastic bag, and puts it outside the door. Cook stands bewildered in his tatty old vest, and now Drake becomes more aggressive.

Right! Let's start your story again, shall we?
Mr Cook I've told you, I don't know nothing!
Drake You don't know nothing. That means you do know something!
Mr Cook Oh, don't start all that double negative crap.
Drake The blood on your shirt.
Mr Cook It's tomato soup.
Drake Blood!
Mr Cook Tomato soup!
Drake Blood!
Mr Cook Tomato soup!
Drake Tomato soup!
Mr Cook Blood!
Drake Aha!!
Mr Cook Okay, so it's blood. No big deal. I stained the shirt doing a job for a mate of mine.
Drake What kind of job?
Mr Cook Plucking pheasants.
Drake *(closing in on Cook, eyeball to eyeball)* You don't look like a pheasant plucker to me.
Mr Cook I'm not a pheasant plucker, I'm a pheasant plucker's mate.
Drake Then why were you plucking pheasants?
Mr Cook 'Cos the pheasant plucker was late!

Drake, having got slightly the worst of the confrontation, now backs off and begins to pace again.

Drake I'm inclined, Mr Cockerel, not to believe a word you've said.
Mr Cook All right. I give in. The stains are, in fact, tomato soup. I dropped some down my shirt while I was in Cook's quarters.
Drake That's more like it! Why don't you just spill the beans, Cook?
Mr Cook I wasn't eating beans, I was eating tomato soup.
Mr Butler Isn't it stimulating to watch the meeting of two great minds?
Mr Gagarin You're not allowed in Cook's quarters, Cook. What's the meaning of it? Up to your old tricks again? You know what mother said!
Mr Cook Yes, yes, I know.

Drake You mean?
Mr Cook Yes.
Drake What?
Mr Cook What?
Drake What do you mean?
Mr Cook I thought you knew.
Drake I was bluffing.
Mr Gagarin Oh, for goodness sake, Inspector, I'll tell you, or we'll be here all night. Some months ago, Cook and Gardner were found together in Cook's quarters - canoodling!
Drake Canoodling?
Plod Like a small boat, sir - very popular with the Eskimos.
Miss Duck That's canoeing, Sergeant.
Drake They were found canoeing in cook's quarters?
Mr Gagarin No, no, Inspector. They were having an affair!
Mr Butler It's actually called a kayak.
Drake An affair's called a kayak?
Mr Butler The small boat popular with the Eskimos.
Drake Have you got all this, Sergeant?
Plod I think so, sir. Cook the gardener was plucking pheasants while Gardner the cook was eating tomato soup with some Eskimos in a kayak, or some such affair, and....
Mr Gagarin Let's just say they were up the creek without a paddle, Inspector, and Mother threatened to sack them if they were ever caught at it again.
Drake Aha! The makings of a motive!
Mr Cook Are you accusing me of murder?
Drake I don't know. Who are you?
Mr Cook Cook, the gardener.
Drake Then I might be. Stick around. Now, let's examine what we have here. *(He struts amongst the characters, confronting the suspects one by one)* We have an old woman, murdered just after 10 o'clock. A business partner, who stands to inherit a prosperous fashion business. A son, who stands to inherit a considerable personal fortune. Two canoeists who were having an affair. And you, Mr Bumfluff - what's your motive?
Mr Butler *(breaking down melodramatically)* All right! All right! I can't stand it any more. Mrs Gagarin was blackmailing me!
Plod Blackmail is a good-looking word, Mr Butler.
Drake Ugly, Sergeant.
Plod Sorry, sir?

Drake Blackmail is an ugly word.

Plod Right, sir.

Mr Gagarin But why, why, why?

Others Yes, why, why, why?

Mr Butler Mrs Gagarin was my old schoolmistress. One day, she caught me behind the bike sheds with a girl called Mary Ship.

Miss Duck Mary Ship - the vicar's daughter?

Mr Butler Yes.

Mr Gagarin Mary Ship. I remember her. So you're Butler the Scuttler!

Mr Butler She swore she'd tell no-one.

Plod You're a sick man. You deserve everything you get.

Plod belts Butler with his truncheon.

Drake *(shocked, averting his eyes)* I didn't see that, Sergeant.

Plod Oh, sorry sir, I'll do it again. *(He does)*

Drake Yes, I got it that time.

Mr Butler *(recovering)* I came here tonight to pay Mrs Gagarin her filthy money, just as I have been doing for the last twenty years. Well how else do you think she became so rich? She was a parasite, living off the one mistake I ever made, when I was just eight years old.

Mr Gagarin There's your motive, Inspector! There's your murderer!

Drake You forget one thing, Mr Gangrene. At the time of the murder, you claim that Mr Butane here was playing bridge, with you!

Mr Gagarin I....er....I wasn't paying that much attention to the game.

Miss Duck No wonder we lost the first rubber.

Plod The first rubber, Duck?

Mr Butler It's a technical term in bridge, Sergeant.

Plod Rubber duck's a technical term in bridge?

Drake Just rubber, Sergeant. Just rubber!

Plod rubs his hands across Miss Duck, who slaps his face. The two stretcher-bearers enter through the French windows. They are carrying a covered body. Drake glances under the blanket, then strides towards Gagarin.

I'm afraid this is going to be very painful, Mr Gondola. *(Drake tweaks Gagarin's ear)*

Mr Gagarin Arrgh!

Drake I warned you. Now, I'm going to need a positive identification.

A Flying Ducks Publication

Mr Gagarin Let's get it over with. *(Drake produces a small photograph from his wallet)* That's Max Bygraves.
Drake Well done. Okay, take her out.

As the stretcher-bearers exit, one of them hands Drake a note.

That's very interesting, thank you. Well, it appears that just before Mrs Gorgonzola died, she scraped two letters in the gravel. A...L.
Mr Gagarin A...L? Alexander! Alexander Guest - the butler!
Drake Well, well, well! Alexander. You little dark horse you. Been murdering old women without telling us have you?
Mr Guest *(not hearing)* What?
Drake Never mind. This particular old woman was unlikely to have referred to her own butler by his Christian name. However...Alison Duck!
Miss Duck Oh, really, this is preposterous! Anyone could have scraped those letters there to put the blame on me.
Plod She's right, sir.
Drake Is she? Is she now? Let's find out. Sergeant - the lie detector.
Plod Sir!

Exit Plod.

Miss Duck Lie detector?!?
Drake A little invention of my own. You've nothing to fear - if you're telling the truth.

Plod enters with the lie detector. It is a ludicrous contraption, with spurious wires, on collapsible tripod legs. Plod continually attempts to set up the contraption, and it continually collapses. Finally, Butler intercedes.

Mr Butler Forget it, Sergeant. You'll never make it stand up in court.
Drake *(embarrassed)* Get rid of it Sergeant.

Plod puts the lie detector outside.

Very well. I'll have to rely on good old-fashioned intuition. *(He strolls along the line of suspects)* The butler did it.
Mr Guest What?
Drake *(raising his voice)* Where were you all evening?

Mr Guest Well, I was alone, on the whole.

Drake Do you often go on the hole alone?

Mr Guest I was in my room most of the evening.

Drake Most of the evening?

Mr Guest Well, I did come to serve drinks to Mrs Gagarin and her guests around nine.

Drake And what time was this?

Mr Guest Er...around nine.

Drake I see. Well, go on!

Mr Guest Well, Mrs Gagarin complained of a headache.

Drake Whose?

Mr Guest Her own.

Drake Got that Sergeant? Sergeant?

Plod is distracted. He has found a goldfish.

Plod Sir! What do you make of this?

Drake Ignore it, Sergeant, it's probably a red herring. Please continue, Mr Ghost.

Mr Guest Guest!

Drake No, I'll come to him later. Now, about this headache.

Mr Guest Oh. Well, Mr Gagarin suggested I go out and get some aspirin from the chemists.

Drake *(pacing)* From the chemists, eh? *(He turns to attack)* At nine o'clock at night??

Mr Gagarin Yes, Inspector. Those are our next door neighbours - Mr and Mrs Chemist.

Drake I see. Carry on, butler.

Mr Butler I'm sorry, I wasn't paying attention. Where were we?

Drake Shut up! *(Pointing to Guest)* You! Had you no aspirin in the house?

Mr Guest I thought we had, but I must have been mistaken. So I went next door, and when I returned, Mrs Gagarin was...dead.

Plod So, you were too late with the aspirin.

Drake She'd been shot, Sergeant.

Plod Oh, right sir.

Drake Who did it?

Mr Guest I don't know.

Drake Oh come now, Mr Gonads! You must have known the old woman better than anyone. Surely you've got a little hunch? *(Plod begins chuckling, but*

Drake remains serious, and his stare quietens him) You must at least have heard the gunshots?

Mr Guest *(not hearing)* What?

Drake Forget it.

Mr Gagarin He would never have heard the shots anyway, Inspector. The next door neighbours are seven miles away.

Drake I see. I don't envy your rates bill, Mr Girocheque.

Mr Gagarin We get by.

Drake You don't seem to remember much about your game of bridge. Were you actually playing when the shots rang out?

Mr Gagarin No, Inspector, that much I can remember. When I heard the shots I was on the phone to the Sergeant here, pledging my annual donation to the Police Ball.

Plod Why, that's right, he was, sir! I heard a shot in the background - a scream - and Mr Gagarin told me to get help right away.

Drake What time was this, Sergeant?

Plod Why, just after ten, sir, like we figured.

Drake Mmm. Very generous of you to pledge your donation once again, Mr Gangley legs.

Mr Gagarin Not at all, Inspector. It's obvious your balls need a bit of support. *(Drake's look says more than words)* Anytime I can lend a helping hand...

Drake Yes well, thank you, Mr Genitals.

Miss Duck makes a move for the door.

Plod Leaving us, Miss Duck?

Miss Duck It is getting rather late, Sergeant, and it's been a tiring day. So if you'll excuse me, I'm turning in.

Duck slinks out of the door.

Mr Gagarin I've asked Miss Duck to stay here tonight, Inspector. I thought it would...er...simplify your investigations.

The phone rings.

Plod I'll get that sir.

Mr Gagarin In fact, you must all be my guests here tonight. It's far too late to travel back to Scotland Yard.

A Flying Ducks Publication

Drake Very hospitable, Mr Gladiator. But we policemen don't actually live at Scotland Yard you know. It's not like Trumpton.

Plod Inspector.

Drake Yes, Sergeant Plod.

Plod For you, sir.

Drake What is it?

Plod It's a telephone, sir.

Drake I see. Excuse me, Mr Goblin. *(He takes the call)* Inspector Drake of Scotland Yard here...*(To Plod)*...It's the forensic report. It appears the bullets were fired by some kind of gun.

Mr Butler My God. The modern criminal doesn't stand a chance with these new laboratory techniques.

Drake Stick at it, boys. *(He puts down the phone)* This could change everything, Sergeant.

Mrs Gardner Inspector, would you mind if we went to bed now?

Drake Madam, I hardly know you!

Mr Gagarin I'm sure we'd all like to get some sleep now, Inspector. We're all very tired. Guest will prepare a room for you and the Sergeant - that's if you've decided to stay.

Drake Very well. I'd like to see you all in here tomorrow at 9 am.

Plod In the morning.

They exchange various "goodnights" and exit, all except Guest, Drake and Plod.

Mr Guest I'll show you to a room, gentlemen.

Drake No, we'll sleep here.

Mr Guest Here?

Drake Here.

Mr Guest Here.

Guest exits.

Plod Here?

Drake Here.

Guest enters with some blankets, and hands them to Drake.

Mr Guest Here!

Drake hands them to Plod.

Drake Here!

The Sergeant places them on the floor.

Plod Here?
Drake I'm getting bored with this conversation, Sergeant.
Mr Guest Hear, hear. Will that be all, sir?
Drake Yes thank you, Mr Geriatric. Goodnight.

Guest exits.

Plod Which side of the floor do you normally sleep on, sir?
Drake Don't make a fuss, Sergeant. There may be a lot of clues right here in this room, and we're going to make sure no-one sneaks in to remove them.
Plod Ah! I'm with you, sir!
Drake Yes, Sergeant, unfortunately you are. *(They begin to prepare for bed)* Tell me, Sergeant - is there a Mrs Plod?
Plod Yes, sir. As a matter of fact, I married her.
Drake When did you first realise you had the brains to be a policeman?
Plod Sorry, sir - I don't understand the question.
Drake Never mind. Try to get some sleep. We have a big day ahead of us tomorrow.

Plod turns off the lights. Drake immediately bangs his head on the warming pan again, and curses silently. Moonlight streams through the French windows and we see the silhouettes of Plod and Drake lie down in their makeshift bed. There is a pause.

Plod Goodnight, sir.
Drake Yes, goodnight, Sergeant.

Another pause.

Plod Sweet dreams.
Drake Shut up, Sergeant.
Plod Yes, sir.

A longer pause.

Plod Give us a kiss. Go on - a nice big wet one...
Drake *(sitting bolt upright in the bed)* Sergeant Plod!!!
Plod *(waking with a start)* Sir!
Drake Kindly remove your hand and get a grip on yourself.
Plod Sorry, sir, I was dreaming. I haven't been feeling myself lately.
Drake Well that's no reason to start on me. Get some sleep.

Pause.

Plod Goodnight, sir.
Drake Yes goodnight, Sergeant!
Plod Sweet dreams.
Drake Shut up, Sergeant!
Plod Yes, sir.

The door creaks open.

Drake Ssssh! There's someone coming!
Plod It's not me, sir.

A figure moves into the room, and the two men pounce, covering the figure with a blanket.

Drake Hit the light switch, Sergeant!
Plod Right, sir!

Plod begins wildly hitting the lightswitch with his truncheon.

Drake Sergeant.
Plod Sir?
Drake Simply switch the lights on.
Plod Right, sir.

Plod switches the lights back on. The bedraggled figure still stands covered by a blanket.

Drake Now! Let's see who we have here!

A Flying Ducks Publication

They whip off the blanket to reveal Guest, extremely dishevelled, but calm.

Plod The butler!
Mr Guest Good morning. Would you care for a cup of tea?
Drake Tea? What time is it?
Mr Guest Eight-thirty, sir.
Drake Sergeant - the curtains.

Plod tears down the curtains and hands them to Drake.

Plod Here they are, sir.
Drake Did you happen to notice what was on the other side of them?
Plod Daylight, sir. He's right. It's morning out there!

Drake hands the torn curtains to a bemused Guest.

Drake Yes, well, there you are. You may go.
Mr Guest Thank you, sir.

Exit Guest.

Plod I don't trust that man, sir. Tell me, how many murder cases have you ever
   been on, in all your years?
Drake Let me see, now, this would be my ninety-third.
Plod Ninety-three cases! And how many times has the butler done it - like in
   the movies?
Drake Life isn't like the movies, Sergeant.
Plod How many times?
Drake Ninety-two.
Plod What does that represent, statistically speaking?
Drake Well, if we ignore this present case, I'd say...one in one.
Plod Impressive odds. My money's on the butler.

Drake holds his head in his hands in despair.

Drake I so much want it not to be the butler.
Plod Sorry, sir?
Drake Forty years I've been doing this job. Forty years! And every time it's the
   butler. The butler. The butler, the damn butler! Well not this time. Not if

I can help it.

Drake has his hands round Plod's throat, squeezing in desperate frustration.

Plod   You can't ignore the facts, sir. The butler is the only one without a motive, and the only one who wasn't here when the murder was committed. It's got to be him.

Drake   *(releasing his grip on Plod)*   You're depressing me, Sergeant.

Plod   Don't you find it strange that he has no aspirin in the house at all?

Drake   *(reaching for the telephone directory)*   What did he say the next-door neighbours were called?

Plod   Err...the Chemists. Mr & Mrs Chemist.

Drake   Let me see now...Chemist...Chemist...damn! Perhaps they're not on the phone.

Drake tosses the directory away, but Plod picks it up and continues the search.

Plod   Here they are, sir! L.G. Kemist!

Drake   Brilliant! Only a policeman would look under K for Chemist. Dial the number.

Plod   Right, sir.

Plod starts to dial a never-ending series of numbers, as Drake paces the room impatiently. Finally, after about one minute and forty numbers, Drake takes the phone from Plod and slams it down. Then he lifts the receiver, dials one number, and speaks instantly.

Drake   Hello? Mr Kemist? Oh. Could I speak to him please? Inspector Drake of Scotland Yard. *(Aside)* It's another damn butler. Hello? I see. Well, there's no need to get him out of bed. Perhaps you can help me. Did you receive a visitor last night? Err...*(grabbing Plod's notes for the name)*...Guest. No, not a guest. A butler. No, not a Mr Butler, a Mr Guest - a butler. No, I haven't been drinking! Shall we start again? *(Aside)* Damn fool butler! Right! Let's start again. I am referring to a Mr Alexander Guest, butler at the household of your next-door neighbours, the Glockenspiels. But surely you must know him - don't you people attend union meetings or something? Aha! And what time did he collect these aspirins? I see. Thank you very much, Mr...er...Mr Shofer. Well, thank you. Goodbye. *(Replacing the receiver)* So, the butler's alibi is confirmed.

A Flying Ducks Publication

Plod By another butler called Shofer. He's probably a murderer too. They're probably in it together.

Drake You mean...two butlers did it? No, I couldn't stand it. I'd resign.

Plod I smell a rat.

Drake *(sniffing)* So do I.

They search around the sofa. Plod raises a rat aloft.

Plod Here's the little critter, sir!

Drake Uggh! This place hasn't been cleaned for months. No real butler would allow a house to get this dirty.

Plod He's an imposter, sir. I'd bet my boots on it.

Drake But if he's not the real butler, there's one person in this house who would know...

Enter Mr Gagarin.

Mr Gagarin Good morning, Inspector, Sergeant. Sleep well?

Plod Yes.

Drake No.

Mr Gagarin Er...good. I presume Guest has offered you tea?

Drake Yes.

Plod No.

Mr Gagarin Er...fine. Good man that Guest. I was very lucky to get him at such short notice.

Drake Short notice?

Mr Gagarin Yes. My other butler clears off one day without so much as an hour's notice. Next day, up pops Guest looking for work. Couldn't believe my luck.

Drake When was this?

Mr Gagarin Oh, a couple of months ago. Of course, it may be a while before Guest totally settles in - after all, Shofer was with us for fifteen years.

Plod Shofer?!

Mr Gagarin Yes, Sidney Shofer - our old butler - good man. Couldn't believe it when he just cleared off like that. Still, mustn't stand around here gossiping. Better let you crack on with your investigations. I'll go and drag the others out of bed.

Exit Gagarin.

A Flying Ducks Publication

Plod Are you thinking what I'm thinking, sir?

Drake I doubt it, Sergeant. Right, let's review the facts. Mrs Gagarin was shot in the cloisters.

Plod I haven't examined the body personally, sir, but it was around that region. The reports says there were five bullets.

Drake Five?

Plod Yes, sir. Two in the back, two in the chest, and one...somewhere else.

Drake Somewhere else, Sergeant?

Plod Let's just say, if she weren't dead, she couldn't sit down.

Drake I see.

Plod And one more bullet sir, right in the clock.

Drake I do wish you wouldn't use such crude language, Sergeant. I know she wasn't exactly good-looking, but...

Plod No, sir, the clock - stopped at 10.03.

Drake Ah, yes. Of course. Six bullets - someone certainly wanted her dead. But who?

Enter Miss Duck. Both her manner and her dress are highly seductive.

Miss Duck Ah, Inspector. Guest told me you'd stayed the night. I was...er...hoping to find you alone.

Drake Sergeant.

Plod Sir?

Drake The young lady was...er...hoping to find me alone.

Plod Oh, that's unfortunate, sir.

Drake Why?

Plod Because I'm here too, sir.

Drake You were here, Sergeant.

Plod When?

Drake Just.

Plod When did I leave?

Drake Now.

Plod Oh! I get it. Perhaps you'd like me to step out of the room for a minute?

Miss Duck Smart man.

Plod Well, there's no need to drop hints, sir. When you want me to go, just say the word. *(He stands his ground rigidly)*

Drake What's the word?

Plod How do you mean, sir?

Miss Duck *(losing patience)* Sod off, Sergeant!

A Flying Ducks Publication

Drake I think that was your cue.

Plod Look, if it's all the same to you, sir, I think I'd like to take a look outside for a while.

Drake Good idea, Sergeant. If you need me, I'll be in here.

Plod Right, sir. And if you need me, I'll be out there.

Drake Right, Sergeant.

Plod Right, sir. *(He still stands his ground, before finally getting the message from Drake's stare)* Oh, right.

Exit Plod.

Drake Good man, Plod. Just lacks one vital organ.

Miss Duck moves towards Drake and begins to wrap herself around him seductively.

Miss Duck Inspector Drake.

Drake Miss Duck.

Miss Duck Birds of a feather, eh, Inspector?

Drake That's er...very good, Miss.

Miss Duck Oh, but I bet you get fed up with bird jokes, don't you Inspector? I get them all the time. People ask how I get my stockings over my webbed feet. They say "I bet you get up at the quack of dawn". You should see restaurant waiters collapse with laughter when I ask for my bill. Then, when I refuse to tip them, they say I'm as tight as a duck's...

Drake Can we change the subject, Miss Duck?

Miss Duck Oh I'm sorry. I didn't mean to embarrass you, Inspector. But Inspector's so formal. Would you mind if I called you Steve?

Drake Not at all. It's better than my real name.

Miss Duck And you shall call me Alison. Oh, Steve, I hardly slept a wink last night thinking about you. You're a man I can trust. Am I a lady you can trust?

She backs him onto the sofa.

Drake Miss Duck - you're squashing my truncheon.

Miss Duck I didn't think Inspectors had truncheons.

Drake Neither did I.

Miss Duck You don't think this murder had anything to do with little old me, do you?

Drake Madam, you're neither old...nor little.

Miss Duck Oh, Steve! There's something very sharp about you.

Drake It's probably my pencil.

Miss Duck It's your mind, Steve. Your mind!

Drake I think we'd better get up now, someone may come.

Miss Duck No-one's likely to come yet.

Drake Oh, you don't know me, Miss Duck.

Miss Duck All right. But first I'm going to steal a kiss.

Drake You'd steal from a policeman?

Miss Duck Oh, Steve!

She smothers him.

Drake Help! Help!

Plod rushes in, and drags off Miss Duck.

Plod You brazen hussy!

Miss Duck All right. So I'm caught committing a crime of passion. What's my punishment to be, Steve?

Plod Steve? But your name's Cecil, sir.

Drake Be quiet, Sergeant Percy Plod!

Miss Duck What's it to be? Interrogation? Torture? Pulling fingernails? The rack?

Drake Don't be obscene. The police department stopped using those sort of tactics six months ago.

Plod September, sir.

Drake That's right. Today we employ subtler methods. It's a battle of wits and intelligence.

Miss Duck And that's where the Sergeant really is in a class of his own.

Plod Let me pull her arms off, sir!

Drake Steady man, steady. Remember the trouble on the picket lines.

Plod *(calming down)* Sorry, sir. I'm all right now. I didn't have to be a policeman you know, I was a very gifted pianist.

Drake Miss Duck, a word in your ear. *(Drake takes Duck to one side, while Plod begins to play an imaginary piano centre-stage)* I'm prepared to overlook this obvious attempt to colour my judgement of this case. But you must take care not to upset Sergeant Plod. He may be no mental gymnast, but he has feelings - he's a human being.

A Flying Ducks Publication

Miss Duck He's a gorilla.
Drake Shhhh!
Miss Duck Sergeant. I'd like to apologise for my remarks. No offence.
Plod That's all right, Miss.
Miss Duck Here, have a banana. *(She reaches for the fruit bowl)*
Plod Oh! Thank you very much, Miss.
Miss Duck It's time the others were here, I'll give them a shout.

Miss Duck opens the door. The others, all listening at the keyhole, fall in in a heap.

Drake Would you care to come in?
Mr Gagarin *(getting up, he offers a cigarette to Drake)* Cigarette, Inspector.
Drake Yes, I know. Sit down, Mr Gravestone.
Mr Gagarin You order me around my own house as if I were a suspect!
Drake Everyone is a suspect, Mr Gob Stopper. Someone in this room is a killer.
Miss Duck How can you be so sure it wasn't an outsider?
Drake Because, Miss Duck, I think Mrs Globe Trotter recognised the killer.
Mr Gagarin Recognised the killer? Inspector, it was very dark that night.
Drake *(he reaches for his hat)* There's more than one way to recognise a killer, Mr Garden Gnome. His face may have been covered like this, *(he covers his face with the hat)* but she still may have recognised his voice.
Mr Butler You're talking through your hat, Inspector.
Drake We'll see, Mr Budgerigar, we'll see. Stand up. Do you promise to tell the whole truth, the truth, er, lots and lots of truth, and more truth than you can shake a stick at?
Mr Butler I do.
Drake You say you were being blackmailed by Mrs Greedyguts?
Mr Butler That's true. The old bag was taking me for a thousand pounds a week!
Drake No further questions. You, Mrs Guard Dog!
Mrs Gardner Me?
Drake Come on, woman, I haven't got all day. Take the stand. Let's hear your story. And take it from the beginning.
Mrs Gardner I was born the daughter of a poor farmer.
Plod *(writing in his notebook)* Your father had no money?
Mrs Gardner Oh, he had loads of money, but he was a lousy farmer.
Plod *(scribbling out the entry in his notebook)* Go on, Miss.
Mrs Gardner My father drank incessantly and continually beat me.

Plod A violent alcoholic!

Mrs Gardner No, he drank water and beat me at chess.

Plod *(ripping the page from his notebook)* Go on.

Mrs Gardner All I had to my name were my old dish-cloth, and the clothes I stood up in, the clothes I went out in, my special low-cut outfits for dinner-parties, and that cheeky Italian off-the-shoulder number...erm...the Land Rover Discovery, a few baubles, and the good fortune to be the first ever National Lottery Jackpot winner.

Plod You poor creature. So how did you become a lowly cook in the employ of Mrs Gagarin?

Mrs Gardner Oh! Terrible misfortune! I put everything on a horse and lost it.

Plod So you're a betting lady?

Mrs Gardner No, I strapped everything to the horse and it ran off.

Plod And you haven't seen the horse since?

Mrs Gardner No, though I've been working my way round rich estates these past three years, checking the stables wherever I go.

Plod Who runs the stables here?

Mrs Gardner The Dutchman.

Others Not the Dutchman!?!

Mrs Gardner Yes.

Plod What's his name, this Dutchman?

Mrs Gardner Van.

Plod Full Name?

Mrs Gardner Truck Van Rental.

Plod Can we speak to him?

Mr Gagarin I sacked him, Sergeant, a week ago.

Plod Oh? And why's that?

Mrs Gardner *(emotional outburst)* He's mean, he is. Just because Van had a cold, he gave him the push!

Mr Gagarin That's not the reason, Mrs Gardner, and you know it! And I won't stand for any more of your impertinence!

Plod So, what's your side of the story, Mr Gagarin?

Mr Gagarin As I explained to the staff at the time very clearly, I dismissed the stableboy because he was feeling a little horse.

Mrs Gardner Same thing!

Plod Do you think you might have antagonised him énough to crave revenge?

Mr Gagarin What are you driving at, Sergeant?

Plod Murder, Mr Gagarin. M-U-R-D-A-H, murder.

Mr Butler Objection!

A Flying Ducks Publication

Drake Over-ruled! Answer the question, Mr Glandular Fever.

Mr Gagarin If he sought revenge, why should the Dutchman attack my frail old mother, and not me? Besides, he was such a quiet, gentle chap. No, it doesn't seem to add up.

Plod Then my suspicions focus firmly back on you and your colleagues.

Mr Gagarin On the other hand I always said he was a murderous swine.

A loud rumble of approval from the rest.

Drake Silence! Mrs Groveller, you may step down. Mr Cooking Oil, if you please.

Cook takes his place centre stage.

Now, Mr Cooking Stove, you said yesterday that at the time of the shooting you were in cook's quarters. She was fixing you a meal of tomato soup, just before she was called to play bridge. Later, when the shots rang out, you spilled the soup down your shirt.

Mr Cook That's right. My only shirt.

Drake Well, we've had that shirt analyzed. Sergeant - the results.

The Sergeant collects a plastic bag from outside the door. It contains a clean white shirt, in two halves. The Sergeant holds up the specimens.

Plod First we tore this badly stained shirt in half. We washed one half in a leading-brand washing powder, the other half in new, improved Bold Automatic. The results?

He hands the shirt halves to Cook, who fondles them.

Mr Cook Well, I've never seen it so clean. That tomato soup really was grimed in, I thought I'd never get the stains out. And as for little Johnney's shorts...

Plod But what about at low temperatures?

Mr Cook Even better. This soup was hot, the label said not, but...

Drake Sergeant Plod! Can we determine the nature of the stains?

Plod Yes, sir. I was coming to that. Bold Automatic is a special laboratory test, and the test proved positive. You see, Bold is an anagram - the stains were indeed...BLOD!

A Flying Ducks Publication

There's a unison gasp.

Drake So! Would you like to change your story, Mr Crook?

Mr Cook Yes please.

Drake Very well, go on.

Mr Cook I was lying.

Mrs Gardner No, Freddie! Don't let them trick you!

Mr Cook It's too late, sweetheart. I'll have to tell them everything! Lillian Gish made her screen debut in 1912. John Keats wrote a poem called Lamia. The bass trombone is equipped with additional tubing to provide...

Drake Er...Mr Clock. I don't think we've got time for you to tell us absolutely everything. Can we stick to the events of last night, in and around this house?

Mr Cook I would have come to that eventually.

Drake No doubt.

Mr Cook Very well. *(Lights dim, spotlight on Cook)* It was just after nine when Mrs Gagarin complained of a headache, and she decided to go for a walk. It was a warm evening, so she'd left the French windows open. A lot of funny things had happened that day. The old woman had been in a foul mood with everyone. She'd found Cook and me canoodling again. She'd had a row with Miss Duck - something to do with the accounts. Mr Butler was here to stay again, and they never got along. She'd even threatened to remove her son from her will, but I don't know what all that was about. I overheard her on the phone to her solicitor. There was a terrible tension in the air. But then...then it happened. You see Inspector, I know who murdered Mrs Gagarin. It...was...

The phone rings. The atmosphere is broken. Drake whimpers in frustration, then moves forward to take the call. During the call, the others, apparently bemused by the delay, casually exit one by one, except for Cook, who stands motionless, and Plod, who is more interested in Drake's conversation, and who therefore doesn't see the others leave.

Drake *(on the phone)* Inspector Drake of Scotland Yard here. Oh. *(He turns from the others and conducts the call sotto voce)* Look, how many times have I told you not to call me when I'm on a case? Now don't start that again. No, look, I stayed here last night...of course I'm sure. No, I didn't go anywhere near Mavis Parson's house. Of course I care about you. No, I can't say that now...well, all right then...you're still Drakey Wakey's little fluffy bottom. *(Plod sniggers loudly)* I must go. I don't know...I'll eat it when I get back. *(The phone is obviously slammed down at the other end. Drake faces the smirking Sergeant)* It was your wife, Sergeant. Now where were we? *(He notices the others have gone)* Well, it seems the others couldn't stand to hear your confession, Mr Cock-a-leeky. Out with it! Who killed the old woman?

Mr Cook collapses, revealing he has a huge dagger in his back. Drake examines a glass Cook was clutching in his hand.

He's been poisoned!

A burst of dramatic music accompanies Drake's and Plod's melodramatic look of horror. Blackout. End of Act One.

ACT TWO

Act Two begins with a re-enactment of the final moments of Act One. Cook, Plod and Drake are on stage.

Drake Now where were we? *(He notices the others have gone)* Well, it seems the others couldn't stand to hear your confession, Mr Cock-a-leeky. Out with it! Who killed the old woman?

Mr Cook collapses, revealing he has a huge dagger in his back. Drake examines a glass Cook was clutching in his hand

He's been shot!

A burst of dramatic music accompanies Drake and Plod's melodramatic look of horror.

Plod Is he dead?
Drake Help me lift him.

They sit him up. Enter Mr Gagarin.

Mr Gagarin Is he dead?
Others Help us lift him.

They raise him to his feet. Enter Mr Butler.

Mr Butler Is he dead?
Others Help us lift him.

They pick his legs off the floor. Enter Mrs Gardner.

Mrs Gardner Is he dead?
Others Help us lift him.

Cook is now dangling precariously above their heads. Enter Miss Duck.

A Flying Ducks Publication

Miss Duck Is he dead?
Others Help us lift him.
Mr Cook Put me down!

In surprise they drop him onto the floor, and gather anxiously round the body.

Drake Listen very carefully. You're going to be all right, but I must know who murdered you. Was it the same person who murdered Mrs Gritwagon? Was it? Who did this to you??
Mr Cook It ...was...

The phone rings again.

Drake I don't believe it! She's done it again! Sergeant, get this man to hospital, I'll deal with this!

Plod drags Cook out by his arms. Cook is writhing in agony.

Miss Duck That's right, Sergeant! Pull his arms off!
Drake *(on the telephone)* Now listen here you miserable lump of whining dung! *(Sudden change of tone)* Good morning, Chief Inspector, and how are you today?

Drake puts the phone down sheepishly.

Mr Butler What did he say?
Drake I'm sacked.

There are barely restrained sniggers from the others.

Mr Gagarin Leave this to me, Drake. I'm not without influence at Scotland Yard you know - my annual donation to the Police Ball sees to that. *(He picks up the phone and begins to dial)* I'm sure the Chief Inspector will see reason - after all, he has a reputation for being a very fair-minded chap. Chief Inspector Bastard please.
Drake This is very good of you, Mr Guillotine.
Mr Gagarin Not at all. Ah! Jack, it's Victor. I'm fine thank you, how are you? Good. And how are all the little Bastards? Good. Look, Jack, I wondered how the arrangements for the Police Ball were coming along. Excellent.

A Flying Ducks Publication

Hope that little cheque for one thousand pounds helped. Yes, I thought it better to make it payable to you personally - cut through the red tape and all that. Oh, Jack, almost forgot. You could do a little something for me. It's about Inspector Drake...*(Gagarin holds the phone from his ear as if to avoid a barrage of abuse)*...yes, quite. But he's making rather good progress here, and I'd hate to see someone as...

Miss Duck Stupid?

Mr Gagarin ...able - someone as able as Inspector Drake removed from the case. So I'd consider it a personal favour if you were to re-instate him. Right. Thanks, Jack. Bye. *(He puts down the phone)*

Drake What did he say?

Mr Gagarin You're sacked.

Mr Butler Your influence at Scotland Yard is awesome.

Mr Gagarin But you're to finish this case first.

Miss Duck Well, well, well. It seems this is to be Inspector Drake's last case.

They all start shaking hands and congratulating a bewildered Drake.

Mr Gagarin Would you care for a small sherry, Inspector? Special occasion.

Drake Well, just a small one, then.

Mr Gagarin Say when.

Gagarin proceeds to fill a pint glass to the top.

Drake That's plenty thanks. Well, bottoms up!

Drake begins to examine his glass, as if he's found something in it.

Mr Butler Anything wrong, Inspector? Found a clue?

Drake *(as if covering up his real discovery)* Er...no, no. Just a small hair.

Mr Gagarin Mrs Gardner, there's a small hair in the Inspector's glass. Please fetch him another one.

Mrs Gardner Another small hair?

Mr Gagarin You just can't get the staff these days.

Mrs Gardner exits with a shrug.

Miss Duck I like a man who can take his drink.

Drake Oh really? What's his name?

A Flying Ducks Publication

Miss Duck George.
Mr Gagarin Inspector Drake. You've been here almost two days now. Do you feel any closer to solving this murder?
Drake Hold my glass for a moment.

Drake hands the glass to Gagarin, then clutches his head in agony and collapses to the ground.

Mr Butler It's the booze. Any minute now he'll be sick.
Mr Gagarin My Persian rug!
Miss Duck Is he dead?
Others Help us lift him!

The previous lifting procedure is followed. Enter Guest.

Mr Guest Is he dead?
Others Help us lift him!

Enter Mrs Gardner with another glass.

Mrs Gardner Is he dead?
Others Help us lift him!

Plod enters to deliver his one line, then quickly withdraws.

Plod Is he dead?
Others Get back to the hospital, Sergeant!
Mr Gagarin Lean him out of the window. That rug cost me an arm and a leg.
Drake I'm not going to be sick!
Mr Gagarin I'm not taking any chances. Mrs Gardner - get a bucket! *(She does)*
Drake Will you listen to me? I'm not going to be sick. Put me down!! *(They drop him to the floor)* I've just got a bit of a headache, that's all.
Mr Gagarin *(producing an aspirin bottle from his pocket)* Would you care for an aspirin? *(Drake reaches for an aspirin - then stops)*
Drake Where did you get those?
Mr Gagarin What?
Drake The aspirin. Your butler said you had none in the house.
Mr Gagarin Ah! Well, there's an easy explanation.

Drake I'm waiting.
Mr Butler Yes, Gagarin, we're all waiting.
Mr Gagarin Well...let's hope the phone rings.

They all stare at the phone, and wait. After about 15 seconds, it rings. A relieved Mr Gagarin answers it.

Mr Gagarin Mr Gagarin's residence. I think it's for you Inspector.
Drake Who is it?
Mr Gagarin God knows. Someone wittering on like a deranged madman.
Drake *(taking the phone)* Yes, Sergeant Plod. Good man! Now, get back here right away! *(Before Drake has even had time to replace the receiver, Plod enters)* Sergeant Plod has just returned from the hospital. Good news. It appears that Mr Cocker Spaniel is going to be okay.

The others stare, without emotion.

Of course, that's not good news to one person in this room. The one who tried to kill him.

They all instantly animate, shouting "Great News" and "Bravo" and "Good Old Cooky".

Now, Mr Guitar Strings. You were explaining about the aspirin.
Mr Gagarin I thought you'd forgotten.
Drake I'm not as stupid as Sergeant Plod looks.
Miss Duck He's right, Victor - you'd better explain.
Mr Gagarin *(with convincing sincerity and reluctance)* I'm sorry Alexander, old chap. I tried my best to cover for you. But it's all over. The Inspector knows you were lying.
Mr Guest *(not hearing)* What?
Drake I checked with the next-door neighbours. Mr Bottletop here did arrive to borrow some aspirin at about 9.20, and left within a few minutes.
Mr Gagarin That's Guest.
Drake No, it's fact! A good detective never relies on guesswork.
Mr Butler Hang on a minute. Old Drakey here's on to something. If the old woman was dead when the butler got back, that means it must have been after ten o'clock.
Miss Duck So?

Mr Butler So, it took him twenty minutes to get next door. And about forty minutes to get back. What on earth was he up to?

Drake *(to Gagarin)* Let me get this clear. You heard the shots at three minutes past ten, and moments later the butler returned.

Mr Gagarin I'm afraid so, Inspector. Look, I had a word with Guest myself before you arrived. He's got no explanation for where he was. He says he came straight back. It's not looking very good for the old chap, is it?

Miss Duck What will he get, Inspector - life imprisonment?

Drake Yes. I would have thought about three months would cover it in his case. However, we're jumping to conclusions again. Notice...*(Drake waves to the oblivious butler, who waves back with his left hand)*...the butler is left-handed. Whereas...Miss Duck! *(Drake feigns a karate chop to Miss Duck's head. She instinctively screams and goes to defend herself by raising her right hand)* Miss Duck is right-handed.

Miss Duck You could have asked.

Drake You might have lied. *(He turns to Gagarin)* And you...

Mr Gagarin Look Drake, before you attempt to karate kick me in the mouth, I'd like to own up to being right-handed too.

Mr Butler So am I.

Mrs Gardner *(raising her left arm first, then swapping uncertainly to the right)* Me too.

Drake I see. That's very interesting.

Mr Butler Well, go on, Inspector. Put us out of our misery. Was the murderer left-handed or right-handed?

Drake How should I know? The old woman was shot.

We hear snoring, and Drake finally notices that Plod is asleep on his feet at the back of the room. Drake grabs a drink and tosses it in Plod's face. Plod wakes with a start, and begins making copious notes. Drake returns the glass and picks up the sherry glass from which he was drinking earlier. Delving into it he finds a number of cocktail sticks.

Here's the reason for my headache. Someone's been spiking my drink. *(Handing the glass to Plod)* Get that fingerprinted, Sergeant.

Plod Sir!

Plod gets a plastic bag from his pocket, tips the liquid into it, hands the glass back to Drake and exits hurriedly, as the drink is leaking from one corner.

A Flying Ducks Publication

Drake There's something very odd going on here. And I'm going to find out what it is. *(He notices a small side door)* What's through here?

Mr Gagarin That's just the coal cellar, Inspector.

Drake The coal cellar.

Mr Gagarin Yes.

Drake You must think I was born yesterday.

Drake exits through the door. We hear a clatter, and he returns, sporting a blackened nose.

Mr Butler Happy birthday for yesterday, Inspector.

Miss Duck It seems that legendary mind of yours is letting you down, Drake.

Drake Say that again.

Miss Duck *(puzzled)* I said, it seems that legendary mind of yours is letting you down, Drake.

Drake watches Duck intently, then examines her teeth as if she were a horse.

Drake Mr Gremlin, how long have you been having an affair with Miss Duck?

Mr Gagarin *(astonished)* How did you know?

Drake The love-bite on your neck - it matches Miss Duck's teeth exactly.

Mr Gagarin You're an observant man, Drake.

Drake It's my job to be observant.

Mr Gagarin *(limping over to Drake)* And now I suppose you'd like to know how I came to have this limp?

Drake What limp?

Mr Gagarin Well, before you ask, yes, it is a gunshot wound - but it was an accident, and it happened a long time ago. You see, I'd left my rifle leaning against a fence, some damn fool animal collided into it, it went off, and...

Miss Duck You may as well tell him, Victor. Inspector, he was shot by a rabbit.

Drake I'm more interested in your relationship, Miss Duck.

Miss Duck I suppose there's no point denying it.

Drake Would you lie to protect him?

Miss Duck No.

Mr Gagarin That's a lie!

Miss Duck Be quiet, I'm trying to protect you.

Drake I see. *(Drake suddenly and dramatically pulls a silly face at Mr Butler, who fails to react)* Observe! Acute myopia!

Mrs Gardner Acute what, sir?

A Flying Ducks Publication

Drake Short-sightedness, Mrs Greasegun. This man can't see any further than his outstretched arm.

Mr Butler The Inspector's quite right. Just after the incident behind the bike sheds, I started to go blind - just as she said I would. All these years I've had to learn to hide my disability, and I thought no-one knew. *(He faces Miss Duck)* How did you know, Inspector? *(Duck points him in the direction of Drake)* How did you know, Inspector?

Drake You're wearing odd shoes. One black, one green.

Mr Butler I could just be weird.

Drake You're that as well.

Mr Gagarin Is any of this relevant? My affair with Miss Duck? Butler's bad eyesight?

Drake Clues. Small clues - but nevertheless significant. My job is to piece the clues together to form a picture of a murderer - or murderess! Tell me, Mr Hand-Grenade, have you got any arms?

Mr Gagarin Yes, Inspector, it's just the way this suit hangs.

Drake Very amusing. *(Drake kicks Gagarin's stick from under him, causing him to fall over)* Now, let's try that again. Have you got any guns?

Mr Gagarin Guns?

Drake Yes, guns. I presume you do have guns in the house? You said you and wild rabbits often went out shooting each other.

Mr Gagarin Ah, guns, guns. It's been such a long time since I've used them. Er, Guest, where do we keep those old guns now?

Mr Guest If you remember, sir, they're in the arsenal, next to your bedroom.

Mr Gagarin Yes, well, thank you, Guest.

There is a clatter off-stage. Plod enters from the coal cellar door, with a blackened nose.

Drake Ah, Sergeant. Just in time. I want you to take the butler here to see the arsenal.

Plod Oh, football fan, eh? Who are they playing?

Drake Never mind. Search upstairs for a gun. Take him with you.

Plod Right, sir.

Plod exits with Guest.

Mr Gagarin If you ask me, Inspector, you're getting absolutely nowhere with this investigation.

Drake I'm not asking you, Mr Gammy Leg.

Mr Gagarin *(turning on Drake in total fury, he prods him backwards with his stick with every word)* Inspector Drake! First of all my name is Gagarin - no Gluesniffer or Gritwagon or Gonad. Secondly, this is my house, and it's my mother that's been murdered, and I'm not having you or your ridiculous buffoon of a Sergeant coming in here ordering me about. Now get this. One more disagreeable word from either of you and, police or no police, I swear I'll take my stick to your concrete skulls and belt your brains out!

The verbal attack leaves everyone speechless. But as Gagarin turns, Drake bobs his tongue out at him. Enter Plod.

Plod What did he say he'd do to us?

Drake Belt our brains out, Sergeant. Nothing you need worry about. I'm prepared to ignore that little outburst, Mr Gonorrhoea. You're understandably a little upset.

Drake ruffles Gagarin's hair affectionately. Miss Duck and Mr Butler have to restrain Gagarin from killing Drake, as Drake turns his back.

Plod Sir, I found this! *(Plod points a gun at Drake)*

Drake Steady, Sergeant! I'll take that. *(He examines the gun)* It seems you're in the clear, Mr Gunslinger. This hasn't been fired for years. I doubt that it even works. *(Drake puts the gun in his pocket, and with a muted bang it goes off. He delivers his next line bravely, through gritted teeth)* Come Sergeant, we have a couple of things to look for.

Plod Like what, sir?

Drake You'll know them when you see them, Sergeant.

They begin searching the room. Plod finds a couple of oranges, and holds them aloft.

Plod Sir?

Drake Bigger than that, Sergeant. *(He spots something behind the settee, and crouches down to examine it)* I've reason to believe that this room is bugged.

Mr Butler Oh, don't be ridiculous, Drake. Now you've gone too far.

Drake Over here, Sergeant! *(They are peering carefully behind the settee. Drake uses his magnifying glass)* See it? There. *(Plod eventually sees it. Drake carefully raises up the object into sight. It is a gigantic microphone, approximately* *four feet long)* Aha! Sshhh! *(Loudly and deliberately)* Nice weather we're having!

Others *(while Drake sneaks towards the door)* Yes. Very nice for the time of year.

Drake swings open the door. Mary Ship, still dressed as a cleaning lady, is lurking behind it, armed with a pistol. In a dramatic struggle Drake finally relieves her of the weapon.

Drake And just who was your next victim going to be?

Mary Ship I ain't killed no-one - honest I ain't.

Mr Butler *(puzzled)* Don't I know you?

Mary Ship No.

Miss Duck Don't I know you?

Mary Ship No. No-one knows me.

Miss Duck A likely story. Take off that pathetic disguise! *(She tears off the apron and scarf, to reveal a scantily clad lady)* It's you!

Mr Butler *(fainting)* Oh, my God!

Drake So! It's you!

Mary Ship Yes.

Drake *(turning to Duck)* Who the hell is it?

Miss Duck That, Inspector, is the reason Mr Butler started to go blind. A young lady by the name of Mary Ship.

Others Mary Ship, the vicar's daughter!

Plod *(grabbing her and shaking her violently)* What were you doing with that gun??

Drake Steady, Sergeant! I'll do the questioning. You're frightening her. *(Grabbing her and shaking her violently)* What were you doing with that gun??

Mary Ship Take your filthy hands off me! *(He does)* Go and wash them first. *(Pointing to Butler, still lying in a faint on the floor)* He's the one I was after. Do you know what he did to me?

Others *(with a childish grin)* Yes!

Mary Ship Oh! How embarrassing! Well, anyway, ever since that day, I swore I'd get even with him.

Drake has slipped on a pair of industrial ear protectors.

Plod What are you doing, sir?

Drake I've heard enough. This poor child has suffered beyond all human imagination. And now, she's paid the penalty for her sins.

Others *(as a negro spiritual response)* Alleluia!

Drake *(pseudo serious)* Promise me you'll never attempt to kill this man again, and I'll let you go. Believe me, he's already paid the penalty for his crime against you.

Mary Ship *(casually)* Okay. Bye!

Others Bye!

Plod Oh, don't forget your gun, Miss!

Plod hands Mary Ship the gun, and she exits.

Miss Duck *(dragging Butler to his feet)* Come on, you can get up now. She's gone.

Mr Butler I'm a monster.

Miss Duck No, just a well-built eight year old.

Mr Gagarin So, Inspector Drake. It's back to the drawing board. Admit it - you've failed!

Drake gets out a pocket calculator, punches in some numbers, then throws it away in despair.

Drake It just doesn't add up. *(He begins to pace)* Something's missing. Something's not right. Sergeant!

Plod Sir?

Drake Let's go over it again. *(They both go over their last few paces as if on a film in reverse, then repeat their previous lines)* Something's missing. Something's not right. Sergeant!

Plod Sir?

Drake No, it wasn't any better that time.

Mr Gagarin Don't take this personally, Inspector Drake, but you're a moron.

Mr Butler Steady on, Gagarin. I'm sure Drakey's doing his best.

Drake It's quite all right, Mr Bric-a-brac. I'm quite used to that sort of abuse. I just take it in my stride. *(As he says "stride" he trips over)*

Miss Duck Are you all right, Steve?

Mr Gagarin Steve?

Drake I'm fine, Miss Duck. Never better. But what have we here? *(He has discovered the reason for his trip - a revolver lying on the carpet)* It seems we have found our murder weapon!

Mrs Gardner It's a gun!

Drake Yes, Mrs Garbage, a gun. Just as the forensic boys said.
Mr Butler That's incredible!
Drake Oh, they're very rarely wrong these days.
Mr Butler No, I mean it's incredible that it could just lie there for nearly two days, without any of us noticing it.
Mr Gagarin Butler's right. Do you think it was planted there?
Drake No, it was just lying on the surface of the carpet.
Mr Gagarin No, no, no. I mean do you think someone put it there?
Drake Well how else do you think it got there, by bus?
Mr Gagarin *(in total frustration, he grabs Drake round the throat, and emits a bellowing scream)* Arrrgh!!!

Plod immediately rushes to Drake's aid, dragging him away.

Drake Sergeant. I'm about to reveal the identity of our murderer.
Plod Our murderer? Have we been murdered?
Drake It's just an expression, Sergeant.
Mr Gagarin Drake, if it means I'll never see you again, take me away. Lock me up. I'll confess to anything.
Drake You can confess all you like. But the fact is, I know that no-one in this room killed the old woman!

There's a dramatic burst of music. Enter Guest.

Ah, the butler. Just in time. Take a seat. Please, sit down, all of you. And I'll explain exactly what happened here last night!!

There's another dramatic burst of music. The curtains close, leaving Plod out front. He turns, and is momentarily baffled by the curtains. He looks for a way through, then finally turns back to the audience.

Plod Well, did you spot all the clues? If you did, and if you're right, then there's a job waiting for you down at Scotland Yard. But the vacancy left by the world's greatest detective isn't going to be an easy one to fill. That's if there is a vacancy. That's if this really is Inspector Drake's Last Case. Confused? Well, as I said before, murder's a funny business. And I hope you heeded the tips I gave you. Don't believe everything you see. Don't always expect a murderer to tell the truth. And make sure you know who's who. If you're still totally baffled, don't worry. Inspector Drake seems to have it all figured out. All you have to do is sit back, watch, and listen. Unfortunately, this is where it starts to get complicated. So, if I might give you amateur sleuths just one final tip. When you're absolutely certain you know what's going on, it's time to change your mind.

The lights dim.

Well, it's getting dark, just as it was that Spring evening, on April 1st. It's nine o'clock. We should be just in time...to witness a murder!

The curtains open. Mrs Gagarin, Mr Butler and Miss Duck are seated, playing bridge. Mr Gagarin is fixing a drink. He pours the contents of a huge bottle, clearly marked POISON, into the drink, and hands it to Mrs Gagarin.

Mr Gagarin There you are, mother, your usual.
Mrs Gagarin Thank you, Vincent.
Mr Gagarin Victor, mother.
Mrs Gagarin What?
Mr Gagarin It's Victor, mother.
Mrs Gagarin What is?
Mr Gagarin My name, mother.
Mrs Gagarin I'm perfectly capable of remembering my own son's name, thank you, Vincent. *(She swigs the drink, and immediately holds her head)* Oh!
Mr Gagarin What is it, Mother?
Mrs Gagarin I have the most dreadful head.
Mr Butler I've always said so.

Enter Guest.

Mr Gagarin Ah, Guest. Mrs Gagarin has a headache. Be good enough to get her some aspirin.
Mr Guest Yes, sir.

Exit Guest.

Mr Gagarin Look, it's a lovely evening, mother. Why not take a stroll in the garden? Do your headache a power of good.
Mrs Gagarin Yes, Vincent. I think I will.
Mr Gagarin Good. Here. *(He hands her a torch he has in readiness behind his*

back. Mrs Gagarin exits through the French windows) After all, I'd hate to get blood on my Persian rug.

Miss Duck What about the butler?

Mr Gagarin Don't worry. *(He produces a bottle of aspirin from his pocket)* Any moment now he'll come through that door and say "Excuse me, sir, but we appear to have no aspirin in the house".

Enter Guest.

Mr Guest Excuse me, sir, but we appear to have no aspirin.

Mr Gagarin *(as if prompting)* In the house.

Mr Guest In the house.

Mr Gagarin You surprise me, Guest. Never mind, pop next door and borrow some from the Kemists.

Mr Guest Yes, sir.

Exit Guest.

Mr Gagarin Right, he's gone for at least half an hour.

Mr Butler What about the cook and the gardener?

Mr Gagarin Don't worry, we have no cook, or gardener. Mother sacked them both this morning.

Miss Duck They were found canoeing again.

Mr Gagarin Canoodling, darling.

Miss Duck Same thing.

Mr Butler Try telling that to the Eskimos.

Mr Gagarin Never mind, let's get this thing over with. *(He goes to a cupboard and produces three revolvers. He hands the first one to Miss Duck)* Here's to a successful business, Miss Duck. *(He hands the second one to Butler)* Here's to being a free man, Mr Butler. *(He raises the third revolver aloft himself)* And here's to a rich inheritance, so richly deserved!

They exit purposefully through the French windows. The lights fade. Curtains close. The silhouetted figure of Mrs Gagarin enters, front of curtains, carrying the lit torch. We see a re-enactment of the opening moments of the play.

Mrs Gagarin Hello? Who's there? I know there's someone there. Come on, who is it? Oh, it's you!

A Flying Ducks Publication

There is a shot, and Mrs Gagarin screams. There are four more shots. The lights come on to reveal Mrs Gagarin slumped over Mr Cook, staining his shirt with blood. Next to Cook is Mrs Gardner, and opposite stand Mr Gagarin, Mr Butler and Miss Duck. They are all carrying revolvers.

Mr Gagarin Cook!
Mr Cook Butler!
Mr Butler Gardner!
Mrs Gardner Duck!

They all instinctively duck.

Mr Gagarin *(to Cook and Gardner)* So, you come back!
Mrs Gardner She made our lives a misery. Ruined us.
Mr Cook A cruel tyrant.
Mr Butler A blackmailer.
Miss Duck And such awful dress sense.
Mr Gagarin My God, look at the time! The butler will be back soon with the aspirin.
Mr Cook I don't think they'll do her any good.
Mr Gagarin *(to Butler and Duck)* You two, inside, quickly. *(They exit)* You two, drag the body into the cloisters, then you'd better get back to your quarters.
Mrs Gardner You mean we're re-instated?
Mr Gagarin As far as I know murder is not a sackable offence. Now get moving.

Gagarin exits. Cook and Gardner drag the body off stage. Curtains open. Butler and Duck enter through the French windows, closely followed by Gagarin.

Quickly, give me those guns. Alison, wind the clock forward half an hour. That damn butler's going to have to account for his time.

Duck winds the clock forward to 10.03. Gagarin fires a shot into it, and puts the other two revolvers away.

Mr Butler What do we do now?
Mr Gagarin Now, we phone the police.
Mr Butler Are you mad?

A Flying Ducks Publication

Mr Gagarin Yes.

Mr Butler Oh.

Mr Gagarin But that's got nothing to do with this phone call. *(He begins to dial)* I think it's about time I pledged my annual donation to the police ball. Ah! Chief Inspector Bastard, please. Oh, I see. When are you expecting him? That's no use. Give me the Sergeant on duty.

Miss Duck Darling, we've just murdered your mother, and now you're calmly pledging money to buy more tracker dogs!

Mr Butler I'm getting out of here!

Mr Gagarin *(pointing the gun)* Oh no you don't! We've got a game of bridge to finish. Ah, Sergeant! Victor Gagarin. Sorry to trouble you so late, but I've done something terribly wrong. *(The others gasp in unison)* Forgot to pledge my annual donation to the police ball. *(The others exhale in relief)* Shall we say...a thousand pounds?

Mr Butler A thousand pounds?

Mr Gagarin Let's call it your final payment - hand it over, Scuttler!

Mr Butler *(handing over a wad of blackened notes)* Here! Have your filthy money.

Mr Gagarin Well, I feel much better now, Sergeant. Now I can sleep. *(Over-deliberately)* Good grief! Is that the time? Three minutes past ten. Better let you get back to work. *(Gagarin suddenly points the gun at Duck, who is standing in front of the French windows)* Duck!

Miss Duck Yes, what is it?

Mr Gagarin No, duck, you idiot!

Duck ducks, and Gagarin fires a shot through the open window. Duck screams.

Sergeant! Sergeant! My mother! She's been shot! Get help, I must go! *(He slams down the phone, with a smile)* Well, I've got the perfect alibi. And the butler's got some explaining to do. Relax. The police are on their way!

There is a harp glissando, and the characters "wobble" to suggest the film convention of the passage of time. During the sequence, Cook, Gardner, Plod and Drake enter. However, during the previous action, the actor playing Drake has disguised himself as authentically as possible as the old hunchbacked butler, Guest. As far as the audience is concerned, therefore, it is Guest who enters, not Drake.

Plod *(narrating to the audience)* And that's the way it happened. An old woman desperately scratches AL in the gravel. But it wasn't Alexander Guest she was trying to write, nor Alison Duck. It was A double L - because they all did it. All, that is, except the butler.

The five suspects rush to produce guns, and chant simultaneously.

Suspects "Okay, Sergeant, you're too clever by half, but you'll never take me alive!"

Plod rushes forward, and they shoot. Plod drops.

Drake *(wielding a machine gun)* Okay, drop your guns!
Plod *(clutching his head)* So! You're not a real butler after all!
Drake That's right!

Drake whips off the disguise, and straightens up.

Others Inspector Drake!
Drake I've been working on this case for months. Are you all right, Sergeant?
Plod Yes, sir. Just a few head wounds. But I don't understand. If you're Inspector Drake, then who was the other chap?

Enter Mrs Gagarin, dressed ludicrously unconvincingly as Inspector Drake, complete with hat and moustache.

Mrs Gagarin You mean me?
Plod My word you've lost weight, sir! It must be the worry.
Drake As I said, I knew that no-one in this room killed the old woman - because the old woman was not dead!

Mrs Gagarin whips off the disguise.

Others Mrs Gagarin!
Mrs Gagarin That's right. *(She hold up a string vest)* Four out of the five bullets were stopped, thanks to this bulletproof vest provided by Inspector Drake.
Plod Would you care to sit down, Mrs Gagarin?
Mrs Gagarin I'd rather not, thank you. Which one of you swines shot me in the butt?
Mr Butler That would be me, Mrs Gagarin. My eyesight isn't what it used to

be. I was aiming for your head.

Mr Gagarin Mother, can I say how glad I am that I really didn't kill you?

Mrs Gagarin Thank you, Vincent. What a comfort it is to have a loving son.
I'll call my lawyer in the morning and arrange to have you put back in my will.

Mr Gagarin You mean, I wouldn't have inherited a penny?

Mrs Gagarin That's right. But that's all in the past. I'll tell the lawyer to leave
all my money to Vincent.

Mr Gagarin Victor, Mother - make sure it's Victor!

Mrs Gagarin And there'll be one million pounds for you, Mr Butler.

Mr Butler One million?

Mrs Gagarin Yes - a thousand pounds a week for twenty years. I'm paying it
all back.

Mr Butler What about interest?

Mrs Gagarin Kiss my ass, Mr Butler.

Mr Butler One million will be fine.

Drake Mrs Gagarin told me weeks ago that she expected an attempt on her life.
We just didn't know who, how, or when. But with Mrs Gagarin playing the
bungling detective, and with me working undercover as the butler, I knew it
wouldn't be long before the culprits made a mistake.

Mr Gagarin I underestimated you, Drake, I thought you were a fool.

Drake *(he begins to stride towards Gagarin, but also towards the warming pan)*
That's exactly what you were supposed to think, Mr...

Mr Gagarin Duck!

Drake Mr Duck. Ummmmph!

Mr Gagarin I did try to warn you, Inspector.

Plod And then, of course, there's the attempted murder of Mr Cook.

Mrs Gardner But he was going to tell you everything. I had to shut him up.

Miss Duck You? But you loved him.

Mrs Gardner A filthy little gardener with one shirt? Never.

Miss Duck I don't understand.

Mrs Gardner And he was a messy eater.

Miss Duck That was blood.

Mrs Gardner It was tomato soup.

Miss Duck It was blood!

Mrs Gardner It was tomato soup!

Miss Duck But the Sergeant said...

Mrs Gardner That's right, the Sergeant said. But it was tomato soup - I saw
him spill it. And I could never love a messy eater. No, there's only one man
I've ever loved. Isn't that right - Sergeant Plod!

A Flying Ducks Publication

Mrs Gardner rips off the Sergeant's moustache.

Others The Dutchman!!
Plod *(instantly attains an accent)* Zat's right.
Mr Butler Nice one Van. That moron act had me fooled. I thought you were a real policeman.
Drake Ever thought of joining the force full-time, Mr Rental? We need men of your calibre.
Plod Well, Mr Drake, I've heard a lot about da big police horses, with da long flowing manes, da big rippling muscles, and ze huge...
Drake Yes, well, thank you, Mr Rental. I'll mention it to the Chief Inspector.

Enter Guest, now transformed into Chief Inspector Bastard. He is carrying a football under one arm, and in his other hand is a briefcase, gift wrapped, with just the handle showing through.

Mr Guest No need, Cecil. I heard every word.
Others Chief Inspector Bastard!
Mr Guest I came right over when I heard the news. Okay, bring him in.

The two stretcher-bearers bring in Cook the gardener.

Others Mr Cook!
Mr Guest No, I checked his fingers. They're no greener than yours or mine. This is not Cook the gardener. But after fifteen years, he just had to be here at the end.
Mr Cook Sorry, Mr Gagarin, they made me do it.
Mr Gagarin Sidney Shofer! My old butler!
Mr Guest Correct. And thank you for bringing him over, Mr & Mrs Kemist. *(The stretcher-bearers nod. Guest hands over the briefcase to Drake)* Oh, Drake, this is for you. A little leaving present from everyone back at the Yard when they heard I'd sacked you.
Drake Thank you. Well, that's another case wrapped up. *(He tosses it away, then points to the football)* Why have you got that?
Mr Guest I thought this was as good a place as any to hold the police ball.
Mr Gagarin Tell me this is all one bad joke.
Others This is all one bad joke.
Mr Gagarin Thank you.
Drake Okay, take them away.

A Flying Ducks Publication

Miss Duck Wait, Inspector.   There's just one thing I don't understand. Gardner's the cook, Cook's the gardener, Butler's the guest and Guest's the butler.   But now you're saying that Sergeant Plod's the Dutchman who's having an affair with Gardner the cook, while Butler the guest is really Butler the Scuttler, but Guest the butler is really Inspector Drake, who turned out to be Mrs Gagarin who's the next-door neighbour of Mr and Mrs Kemist who are holding Cook the gardener who's really Shofer the butler.   Right?
Drake Erm. That's about the size of it, yes.
Miss Duck Well in that case..

The whole cast turns to the audience and points.

All Who are you???

Lights to black.   Curtain.   Take a well-earned bow.

A Flying Ducks Publication

PROPS

PERSONAL PROPS:

Sergeant Plod Torch, truncheon, note-pad, wristwatch, 2 plastic bags.
Mrs Gagarin Torch.
Mr Gagarin Walking stick, cigarettes, bottle of aspirin.
Inspector Drake Magnifying glass *(with no lens)*, photograph in wallet, hat, ear protectors, pocket calculator.
Miss Duck Mud on heel, cigarette and holder.
Mr Guest Ear-trumpet.
Mr Cook NB: Dagger in back - end of Act One.

ON STAGE: Rug, poker lying on floor, low-hanging bed warming pan, bullet hidden in grandfather clock, goldfish *(with or without bowl)*, telephone and telephone directory, rubber rat on settee, large dusty book, drinks table with drinks including sherry bottle and pint glass containing cocktail sticks, large dummy microphone hidden behind the settee, a gun lying on the rug.

OFF STAGE: Hoover, stretcher with covered body, lie detector, blankets, clean white shirt in two halves in a plastic bag, glass, bucket, gun *(brought in from the cellar door by Plod)*, pistol *(brought in by Mary Ship)*, machine gun for Drake, gift-wrapped briefcase and football for Chief Inspector Bastard, string vest for Mrs Gagarin.

SPECIFIC TO FLASHBACK IN ACT TWO.

Guns for Cook and Gardner.
Large bottle marked poison.
Three guns in cupboard.
Pack of cards.
Small cards table.
Wad of blackened notes for Mr Butler.
Torch for Mr Gagarin.

LIGHTING PLOT

ACT ONE:

Cue 1:   Spotlight on Plod, centre stage.
Cue 2:   Spotlight dims to black.
Cue 3:   Full interior lights at night. Moonlight through french windows.
Cue 4:   Interior lights off, moonlight through french windows.
Cue 5:   Interior lights back on. Moonlight through french windows, cross fades to daylight.
Cue 6:   Lights dim to centre spotlight on Mr Cook.
Cue 7:   Lights back up to full interior.
Cue 8:   Lights to black.

ACT TWO:

Cue 9:   Lights up from black.
Cue 10:   Lights dim to black. *(Plod in front of curtains)*
Cue 11:   Lights to full interior. *(Flashback)*
Cue 12:   Lights fade to black. *(Garden scene)*
Cue 13:   Lights up gently to show killers in garden after shooting.
Cue 14:   Lights to full interior as killers re-enter room.
Cue 15:   Lights "wobble" to suggest passage of time.
Cue 16:   Lights to black at end.

EFFECTS PLOT

ACT ONE:

Cue 1:   PLOD: "Inspector Drake's last case?" Burst of dramatic music.

Cue 2:   MRS GAGARIN: "Oh, it's you". Gunshot, followed by four more shots, then dramatic music.

Cue 3:   PLOD: "I think I can hear Inspector Drake coming now." High pitched squeal of tyres, car door slam, footsteps running up gravel.

Cue 4:   MR BUTLER GETS UP. Sound of very loud hoover.

Cue 5:   MR GAGARIN: "Simplify your investigations..." Phone rings.

Cue 6:   COOK: "It was..." Phone rings.

Cue 7:   DRAKE: "He's been poisoned!" Dramatic Music.

ACT TWO:

Cue 8:   DRAKE: "He's been shot..." Dramatic music, as cue 7.

Cue 9:   COOK: "It was..." Phone rings.

Cue 10:   MR GAGARIN: "Let's hope the phone rings..." Phone rings.

Cue 11:   DRAKE EXITS THROUGH CELLAR DOOR. Clatter from cellar.

Cue 12:   MR GAGARIN: "Thank you Guest..." Clatter from cellar.

Cue 13:   DRAKE: "Killed the old woman..." Dramatic music.

Cue 14:   DRAKE: "happened here last night..." Dramatic music.

Cue 15:   MRS GAGARIN: "Oh, it's you..." Repeat of cue 2.

Cue 16:   MR GAGARIN: "The police are on their way..." Harp glissando, to mark the passage of time.

Other music stabs and links optional.

Try another Flying Ducks Publication!

You'll find details of all the comedies, including sneak previews of the scripts, video extracts, specially created sound effects and the online bookshop, all on the theatre page of our web site:

www.flyingducks.biz